The
Path
to
Mastership

Books by John-Roger

Spiritual Warrior—The Art of Spiritual Success
Inner Worlds of Meditation
The Tao of Spirit
Forgiveness: The Key to the Kingdom
The Christ Within & The Disciples of Christ
    with the Cosmic Christ Calendar
Dream Voyages
Walking with the Lord
God Is Your Partner
Q&A from the Heart
Passage Into Spirit
Relationships—The Art of Making Life Work
Loving—Each Day
Wealth & Higher Consciousness
The Power Within You
The Spiritual Promise
The Spiritual Family
The Sound Current
The Signs of the Times
The Way Out Book
Sex, Spirit & You
Possessions, Projections & Entities
Music is the Message
The Master Chohans of the Color Rays
Manual on Using the Light
The Journey of a Soul
Dynamics of the Lower Self
Drugs
The Consciousness of Soul
Buddha Consciousness
Blessings of Light
Baraka
Awakening Into Light

For further information, please contact:
Mandeville Press®
P.O. Box 513935
Los Angeles, CA 90051-1935
(213) 737-4055

The Path to Mastership

JOHN - ROGER

M

Mandeville Press
Los Angeles, California

Published by Mandeville Press
P.O. Box 3935
Los Angeles, CA 90051

Printed in the United States of America

I.S.B.N. 0-914829-16-5

Contents

1
The Path
Upward

If you look for what is beautiful in everything that happens, you'll find the secret of the great spiritual Masters, which is that everything is in its right and proper place, even if you cannot see it yet. You can exercise the consciousness of mastership in a most dynamic way by saying, "Father, Mother, God, I ask for the highest good of all concerned to be brought forward." When you ask for the highest good in the name of the Christ, the Mystical Traveler, the Preceptor, or God, it will work for you. When you ask within your own Christed Light, the Light of your Soul, you can also be in very good territory because it will be done as you see it through Spirit.

The path to mastership can appear very narrow. The boundary lines may seem to be set very close together—not so close that a universe cannot walk through them, but so close you have to keep yourself within the universe. As you ask, "Father, where is truth?"—that question being the first step on the path—the world starts to unfold because you have opened yourself to the Light and asked it to come into your life. You have knocked, and the door will open to you. As you seek the truth in your life, other steps along the path unfold to you, and you find yourself moving closer and closer to Spirit in a very natural and automatic way. There is nothing strange about this path. There is nothing unusual or unnatural. Spirituality is the most natural expression in the world. It is your true and abiding nature.

Those of you who work in the Movement of Spiritual Inner Awareness have the absolute freedom to go where you want, do what you want, believe what you want, test whom you want, and doubt whom you want. It's all right with me. I am going to continually maintain my levels of awareness. And it just so happens that when I maintain mine, the people who are working with me can maintain theirs much more readily because the Mystical Traveler Consciousness, which is *truth, sacrifice, faith, creativity, intelligence, will, devotion, discipline, service, love, and MASTERSHIP,* will maintain the focus of Spirit for all. You can move your whole consciousness forward by developing these eleven key traits which define the path of mastership.

If you get one of these eleven key traits of mastership functioning in your consciousness, all the others will start coming into line. Then you move into mastership by connecting with one who is a force of Light or by moving into your own levels of mastership. You may master your imagination or your desires and lusts

2

so they do not control your life. There are a lot of areas you might want to master. You might bypass all the games and go on to greater things.

One thing that will tend to block spiritual uplift-ment is *boredom*. If you start getting bored, you find you are no longer in a Master's consciousness. You have ceased to be responsible for your own actions and your own mental and physical health and vitality and have said, "Do it for me; make me feel good or I'll get bored." You might learn something from being bored. And if you do, it'll be a positive action for your growth.

Jesus talked about the path to mastership in a very simple way, saying, "Seek ye the kingdom of God, and all these things shall be added unto you." (Luke 12:31) Living the steps of mastership will lead you to the kingdom of God.

TRUTH

There are two truths: an outer truth we call objective truth, and an inner truth we call subjective truth. The inner truth may represent a greater truth than the outer truth because the outer truth is usually in a constant state of change, while the inner truth may be in a state of movement, but not necessarily change.

Many people have asked, "What is truth?" My definition of truth is anything that leads you to God. An illusion will not get you to God; it will take you on a side trip. *Eventually,* everything, even illusions, will direct you back to the truth and to God, but it will take you a little longer. You're moving toward that Oneness of consciousness called God whether you are

3

momentarily working in truth or illusion. So it's easy to say that truth is everywhere. It is, but it depends on how you look at it. It depends on who you are, where you grew up, your religious training, and so forth. There are a lot of truths. The truth of today may have to be modified or changed tomorrow as you acquire new information. So, based upon the new information, you discover a new truth. You are always looking for what is true and moving toward that, because in a state of truth there is security and an underlying buoyancy where no matter what happens, you can say, "I know." This is not the conceit of "I want you to think I know," but the knowing that says, "I don't care what you say or think; you can do as you please, I know this is so." That truth cannot be shaken or thrown down. That truth does not have to be defended or protected; it stands.

When you reside in the truth of your own conscience, you don't have to defend yourself. If you find you must defend yourself, it may be because you are standing in an illusion. So check carefully and ask yourself if you are working in areas of illusion or truth. If it turns out that you're working in illusion, you may want to change and bring more truth into you. In truth, there is no deviation from perfection. Perfection has a very wide scope, sure, but no "exclusion" or prejudgment. Truth recognizes that you are expressing the eternal movement, the eternal cosmogony of life as you flow from point to point. You don't have to defend the car you're driving as being the best or worst. If that's your car at the moment, you just go ahead and flow with it. It serves the purpose of moving you through this physical world of reflected Light.

SACRIFICE

The thing that's interesting about truth is that you may have to sacrifice part of what you call truth to fulfill another part of what you call truth. At some point in your search for truth, you will place some things in a subordinate position to others. An example might be that although it's _true_ you love to go out dancing until three in the morning, it's also _true_ that going to bed earlier means doing better work the next day. So you give up one aspect of what is true to gain another. You may say, "Yes, it was fine to run around town when I was younger, but now those things must go. I must sacrifice to reach into new and greater things which hold promise for me." Whether or not that promise is a spiritual promise, you have to decide.

The state of sacrifice can be a beautiful thing. Maybe you give up that ten o'clock television show to do your spiritual exercises. Or you give up the Tuesday night poker game to go to a class or seminar, knowing that you're going to find some advancement or enlightenment. Sometimes you enter into "sacrifice" on the faith of what you've seen other people gain. People who were "boozing it up" or "getting loaded" just as often as you were, come into a more balanced expression. You notice they're not expressing themselves through drinking or drugs any longer, and they seem happier. So you enter into faith that these changes can happen to you also.

As you work in truth, you sacrifice relative truth, always with the faith that you will find a more exacting and fulfilling truth. Then you find yourself on a spiritual path, seeking truth, sacrificing those things which are not true, and having the faith that you can find those things which are true for all people. You enter into a great sense of creativity, allowing each person to create for himself beautiful things which last and endure as truth.

It's very easy to follow the truth, but it can be very difficult to *discern* the truth. Or we could say it's very easy to follow a wise man, but a wise man is hard to find. When you find the truth, the wise man, or the Light, have the wit to follow and to be creative in your approach. Work with the truth to see what you can build with it; see what the limits of your own expression are. If you're involved in something that has boundary lines or limitations, be careful because someone outside that dimension may look at your action and say, "That's not true; that is not truth." And you find yourself back in the area of relative truth.

FAITH

Relative truth can be tricky. For example, if I told you the sun wasn't going to come up tomorrow, you might dismiss me as a false prophet. Of course, there is no real guarantee that the sun will come up tomorrow, but in a *faith* area you know it will. You *know,* and this type of faith becomes so strong nothing can shake it. But if I put you deep in a hole in the ground and shut out the light, the sun wouldn't come up for *you.* That's subjective truth coming in. So you always have to qualify your statements, which keeps your consciousness moving. You don't hold to a rigid point, like, "I've got it; this is it; no other way works." Rather, you say, "This way is working right now." And if it's working ten minutes from now, keep working with it. But if it stops working, move on to something else because it will no longer be true for you. When you reach the Supreme God, you won't be working in transitory truths. But until you do find God, you will be working in areas of relative truth because you have no other choice. Work them beautifully while you are here.

CREATIVITY

After you have entered into the areas of faith and acceptance and have learned to flow with that which is, you may start to feel a great urging within you. Something says, "Let's do things. Let's accomplish. Let's become creative." You may feel artistic expression flowing through you, and you might want to grab a paintbrush and paint. You might want to clean or fix up the house or do the laundry. You might want to go surfing to see if you can do something greater than ever before. You might want to design some new clothes for your family or cook some new dishes for dinner. There are lots of creative expressions that are available to everyone.

As your creativity comes forward, you want to give into life. You take from life, sure, and life is here to be taken from, but it's also here to be given to. So you get a chance to enter into creativity. In creative endeavor, your intelligence is stimulated. You may see a picture and say, "Oh, what a fantastic idea," and your mind opens, and you have fourteen new ideas because the *intelligence* came in. Sometimes I'll talk to people about a certain idea and see their consciousnesses unfold and expand as more ideas come forward. My creative approach to a concept may cause them to suddenly see all sorts of other possibilities. Intelligence and creativity move together.

INTELLIGENCE

As your consciousness opens to new concepts, you are entering into the area of intelligence. You may study, search, read the works of the great philosophers, and study with the great teachers. Your quest is for that which will work for you. You may read the works of the great historical philosophers and say, "But I don't believe that." Yet they wrote it as truth, as an avenue or expression of truth as they knew it. You may come to the point where you don't want to study other philosophies because you don't want their truth. You want your own truth. Many people say, "I don't want to study history because I think a lot of people lied when they wrote things down; they were prejudiced and untruthful and didn't record it the way it was. They wrote it from a prejudiced point of view and I don't want that. I want to see the truth. Dear God, I don't want lies. I can lie to myself, but I don't want to do that. I want to know the truth." To discern truth, you can use your intelligence. Intelligence is the key to bypass your hangups and move into what is without judgments, prejudice, or the idea of personal gain.

When the Light descends in your consciousness, it allows you to reach into the "hope chest" and bring forward those ideas which will work for you—ideas which you can use later because your intelligence will still be in those areas. I'm not talking about mentalizing, which is more of a "record/play back" process. I'm talking about the ability to take idea "A," idea "B," and idea "C" and, within yourself, jump over to "H" and create a whole new process. This is the type of intelligence that makes it possible for people to find their own way once they have been shown the Light.

With intelligence you can bypass your prejudice. You'll know what it is, but you'll be able to hold it in line and consciously move where you wish. This process is more than using your brain. It is the Soul bringing forth its intelligence. When you get an intuitive "I see it" understanding, that's the Soul passing the spiritual energy right through the mind as intelligence. The more you can move into the Soul and bring it forward, the higher you go each day. As you feel yourself beginning to lift into Soul consciousness, if you bring your mind in, you'll bring yourself right back down here to the "tiddly-wink" games of the physical level. The trick is to just keep doing and moving forward into each new moment.

WILL

As you use your intelligence to perceive more clearly and begin to decide what you will do to increase your awareness and further your progression, you may begin to assert your will by saying, "I *will* do this. I *will* do that." To assert the will is fine, as long as it is useful to you. Some people become very "willful" and turn away from the positive expression saying, "I *won't* do that. I don't care if you say it's good for me. I *won't* do it." They move into the shadows of their own consciousness and become very frightened as their will backfires on them. You can create monsters in your mind who lie and wait for a chink to appear in the "armor" and then attack—usually when you're alone or when you're not really sure of what's happening. Your will isn't too helpful to you at those particular times.

When will fails, you say, "Oh, God, what do I do now? I insisted on my way, not Spirit's. Now I'm doing it my way and everything is falling on my head." When you decide you *will* do something, you often botch that area because you become possessive and tell people, "You will do it my way or else." They're probably ready to take the "or else" just for the fun of it. Your challenge is to make your will useful to you, not to let it stand in your way. But it's very easy to get trapped by the will and say, "You didn't do it my way; get away from me. I hope I never see you again." If you place this type of action in motion, you're most certainly going to be incarnating back to balance that action. Those negative expressions have to be worked out and resolved. Make your will useful to you. Make it flow toward your divine destiny.

A certain Light quality resides within each person. Using your will, you can bring the Light forward in more complete ways. Then your will has become useful to you because it has taken you deeper and further into the consciousness of God, the One God who resides both within you and in objective reality. Then when you say, "Father, Thy will be done," you are saying, "Your will through me becomes One will, and I give it to you." Your will has become useful to you because you're moving it toward ultimate truth. It becomes easy to sacrifice your own beliefs about what must be the right way to the greater idea that all things are right and proper.

Many times when you say, "Everything just really went badly today," we say, "Did it really go that badly? Or were you placed in a protective blessing so that you didn't fall into the abyss in another area?" You may say, "I don't know. Maybe, maybe not." Where *is* your faith that everything is right and proper in God's holy thoughts? As you exercise and move back into your faith, you start becoming creative again; the intelligence flows, and the will comes forward to blend with the Father's will, and finally you say, "Oh, Father, Thy *will* be done on earth as it is in heaven."

DEVOTION

As your will and the Father's will become one, you enter into that quality of devotion that gives the credit to Spirit. You know that of yourself, you can do nothing. You say, "Father, here I am. This is your child. Whatever you have for me to do, I will do gladly, because I know I'm going to inherit all things. If I have to inherit the manure pile before I inherit the flower garden, so be it. Or if I inherit the flower garden and then the manure pile, that's okay, too. However you see it, Father, I'll abide by Thy will."

Be very thankful you can grow regardless of any physical, mental, emotional or financial situation. Your devotion to God can transcend all situations and become the constant factor of your life. Then you follow one Light, the Light which is God. It's been called many names and worshipped in many ways, but everyone is reaching to this one consciousness. There is one mind, the mind of God. There is one consciousness, God consciousness. All else are tributaries of the One. If you can get on a tributary leading back to God, you can follow it back into the *mainstream* of God's energy. The Movement of Spiritual Inner Awareness is in the mainstream. It has been demonstrated over and over again. The Light has been demonstrated beyond a mental or emotional process. When you stop mentalizing and ask from your heart for

Spirit's "Light" to be with you, things around you change. Then you *know* those things which seemed so locked in and crystallized can be released and altered. It's a great day when you recognize that the things in your life which seemed inalterable can be lifted.

When your life is not going too well, you may enter into the area of devotion, saying, "Father, help me. God, save me. Deliver me from my enemies." You enter into extreme devotion based upon great emotional concern, which would be all right if that devotion were focused toward locating the truth within yourself and sacrificing the truths which don't work for you. Be devoted to faithfully finding new truths and to creating and building on those areas of truth. Then look through your intelligence at what you have learned to see how you stand. By these processes, you make your will useful to you and grow to be very devoted to the freedom of your own expression.

Devotion may express itself as, "Lord, here I am to help, to be helped, to share and to be one with all. I don't have to be all things to all people. I'm not even going to try. I'm just going to be me." Just to be you can be a great challenge. I've said so often and to so many people, "Thank God you're you." And they look at me and think, "Thank God I'm me? But I'm so angry and hurt inside." That's not the part I see. That's the illusionary part which is always changing. You'll sacrifice it later when you realize truth isn't going to reach into those areas. You'll sacrifice it when you get the vision of a greater reality.

Your devotion keeps you moving forward. All you have to do, believe it or not, is keep yourself centered toward the Light consciousness. It's easy. Everyday in every way, turn toward the Light. Ask for the Light in the morning when you get up, when you get to the car, when you get to the gas station, before you get on the freeway, when you park your car, and on the way into work. You'll enhance your realization of Living In God's Holy Thoughts. That's the Light—all the time. The more you attune to it, the more your inner Light grows until one day you say, "I am the Light," and it's not a lie. You say it because it is so. Yet something inside of you will be so humble that you may keep this fact to yourself. But when someone asks, you must truthfully acknowledge that you are the Light. Yet as you hear it, you say, "Yes, that *is* the truth, but you are also the Light. Everyone is." The Light holds you to the truth, and that becomes a great joy.

DISCIPLINE

As you enter into the idea of being devoted to someone, whether it's to God, the Light, your husband, your wife, your parents, your children, or your job, you find out that almost automatically you start disciplining yourself into those things which will lead you higher. The discipline pulls in your boundary lines so you're not spread too thin. You become more self directed. You hold yourself in line and give up a lot of things you used to think you really wanted. You ask yourself if those things are really on your path of truth and Light. If you hear, "yes," move into it; if you hear, "no," move out of it. And you develop the wit to discern the inner direction.

As you start pulling in the boundary lines, you

13

start feeling very strong. Your discipline becomes so good that you can stop overeating, put down the cigarettes, control your temper, or take charge of a lot of other areas. You may be more honest in your life and relationships. You may say, "I'm not going to be dishonest any longer." Are you aware that dishonesty forfeits divine aid? Are you going to give up the Kingdom of God for thirty-five dollars? You might as well take thirty pieces of silver and hang yourself. That sounds ridiculous, yet you may see your relationship to your integrity in more subtle, though not dissimilar, ways.

I have been offered rather large sums of money, believe it or not, to spy on industry, to tap into what is happening in someone's engineering department. My answer has always been, *and always will be,* "No!" To violate the consciousness of any person or any group would put me back on the "wheel of eighty-four," the cycle of reincarnation. I'm free of incarnation patterns at this point. I've completed those cycles. There is no need for me to go back again.

When you know the Light, no one will be able to buy you with a little piece of green paper with fancy designs on it. Some people may bow down and worship the dollar, but who wants to do that when you can have the sustaining energy of God's Light and love. When you find that, you find your discipline taking place automatically. You start doing things in a right way, in a right consciousness. You don't even have to make an effort. If you experience doubt, you hold. If you don't have the information necessary to make a decision, you just hold until you do. If you ask for the Light and God's guidance and get no directive, you just hold. When you hear the inner direction, you can say, "Okay, now I can do it."

SERVICE

As you develop discipline and become more and more attuned with the Light, something inside of you says, "I want to be of service. I want to help. Father, how can I help?" And the answer may come forward, "You're a channel for the Light. Go forward and do God's work. You don't have to do missionary work. Just open yourself and let the Light flow through you. Let Me do My work through you; glorify My work and give all the credit to Me." That's easy. God is doing the work. To be able to serve Spirit is a great blessing. When you have asked Spirit to be of service, you may find someone such as your retired parents, an infirmed cousin, or an orphan off the street coming to you and asking, "Will you put me up for awhile?" Maybe that is how you are to serve. Sometimes another person's illness is an opportunity for you to serve. Those who sit very quietly in the silence that roars the name of the Light and do the most mundane jobs in love and devotion are performing a beautiful service that God sees as very great, indeed.

LOVE

About the time you move into the consciousness of service, you start realizing that the first thing you have to do is TO LOVE. When you love, you don't look at anything as being a burden or a sacrifice, and you may not be overly concerned about the truth. And when you love, you're in an area of faith all the time, the living faith which is demonstrated continually. In love you don't even have to use the intelligence. Through divine love you will see all things in proper perspective, and you use your will only to recognize it. Your love becomes devotion, "I love you. God bless you." You can even bypass the area of discipline and enter directly into the area of divine service to become part of the living free.

The quality of divine love sustains, holds and supplies you with all things. It comes in as a great rhythm and movement and fills your cup to overflowing. Love floods through you, and all you can think of doing is demonstrating it. So you say, "Father, I'd like to be of greater service. Here are my abilities, my talents, my life expressions. Do with them what you want." Life smooths out, and you start having such a good time that you say, "Is this all there is to it? It's so easy; it's so free!"

MASTERSHIP

Then along comes someone who plays a different tune and marches to a different drummer. You meet one who ascends to Spirit and who also touches back to this planet with a master Light energy. At that point, you either meet a Master, become a Master, or enter into masterful expression. You experience the blessings and the grace of God as a direct line, a direct link, a direct connection into your consciousness.

As you meet a spiritual Master, you are known through his consciousness into the Godhead. Everything you say to the Master flows into the universe, and the things you do in the name of the

16

Light flood to those other universes and are recorded in Spirit. The joy within you sustains you here as it takes you higher, deeper, and into even greater fulfillment. All you've worked for over the years comes into culmination; you enter the Master's path. The karmic burdens which have confined you to these lower levels are rapidly dissolved. They may even be changed from a debit to a credit, so that most of the things you have done become a *credit* to your existence.

Your "sins" are now transformed into the positive stepping stones of experience, and you find yourself lifting into greater and greater awareness of Spirit. The way opens and unfolds, the way that has always been prepared for you. You just have to walk it, just *be* it and be open. And you love with a whole different quality. As you lose the personal love you've felt for special people, you enter into a greater impersonal love which loves everyone perfectly and never interferes.

Many people, when they look upon a Master, experience the *Darshan,* which is an immediate elevation of consciousness. Some people may look upon a Master but are not allowed to see the greater Light because they have many things yet to work through. They can, in a sense, live right next door to a Master of Light and never know it until the Master shows himself in spiritual reality. There are many Masters of Light on the planet. There are very few that can give you the keys to your own Soul development.

Each person has to decide how they're going to awaken themselves to Spirit. You will awaken. There is no question about that. *When* you awaken is your choice. Spirit does not push or urge. You could embody back on this planet ten million times, and it all takes place right now as far as Spirit is concerned. That's why it is perfect. That's why there are really no catastrophes or disasters. There is only man's interpretation of events, and how you choose to interpret them helps determine how you act toward them.

When you enter onto a Master's path, either you master it or it masters you. There is no neutral ground. A lot of people have said, "Oh, I would like to be a Master." And I say, "That's fine. It's a very commendable idea. Do you know what it represents?" They may think they won't have to do anything anymore. But as long as you are in a physical body, you have to stay masterful; you have to continually hold to the iron rod of your own beingness because you _can_ move off the Master's path.

THE DOWNWARD PATH

What would be the qualities of moving off the Master's path? The _love_ changes and becomes a controlling love, which expresses, "Do what I want you to do." Even as you say, "I don't care what you do; you can do what you want," something inside you says, "But not _that_." You will feel it. Your loved one's expression becomes a burden and an oppression to you, and you say, "Leave me alone. Just go away." Then, rather than living in an attitude of _service_, you find yourself saying, "You've become a burden to me. You're my yoke, my ball and chain." Then your idea of _discipline_ shifts, and you say, "I'm going to do just as I please; just leave me alone, and don't go checking on me because what I do is none of your business. If I feel like I want to go down and get drunk, I'm going to do it." Then the idea of _devotion_ changes, and you find out you're really devoted to nothing, not even yourself. Then your _will_ comes in, and you say, "I will not do that, and I don't want you to do it either." And you know right then and there that you are off the Master's path. You can feel it slip. Your _intelligence_ becomes mentalizing: "But you said; I heard you say....." Your _creativity_ becomes destructive. You say, "That's no good. That's terrible. Why bother?" You may try to block the _faith_ of another person to hurt them, to make them lose the vision of who they are. And you _sacrifice_ everybody else to your ego-emotional point of view. Even the _truth_ becomes an illusion, and you try to get away with all you can. At this particular point, truth eludes you and you step back into the illusion of reembodiment. The path is pretty clear. The rungs of the ladder you ascend are the same rungs on which you descend.

There is room at the top because a lot of people get there and go back down the other side. As long as you reside in your physical body, you must continually exercise your living-free consciousness. You can choose whatever you choose, go wherever you go, and do whatever you do. It's important to allow everyone else that same freedom of expression.

The process of mastering—expressing, refining, and perfecting—is continuous. The choice of following the upward path or the downward path presents itself to you many, many times each day. You get the chance to choose _for_ Spirit or _for_ worldly concerns. When you demonstrate mastership, no one can take it away from you. You secure your position by demonstrating the consciousness of it. In the same way, no one can *place* you in a position of mastership if you have not earned it. There is no way to deceive the Spirit. There is no way to deceive God. As you demonstrate your ability to discern truth, to sacrifice the lesser worlds for the greater Spirit, to live in faith and creativity, to make your intelligence and will useful to you, and to be devoted and disciplined in loving service to all, you have anointed yourself in mastership. Others can only reflect to you that you are there. And if you are there, of course, it does not matter what anyone else says or thinks. So ultimately it comes right back to: "To thine own Self be true."

2
The Path
of Initiation

The Sound Current is the audible stream of Light that flows from the God Source through all levels and into physical consciousness. When you follow the path of initiation into the Sound Current, you travel or "ride" the Sound Current from these worlds back into the God Source. It is very simple to do, although it is not necessarily easy because you are so conditioned to the illusion and maya of the lower world. The eleven steps to mastership will prepare you to hold the focus of Spirit and allow you to enter into the path of initiation.

The paradox of the Sound Current is that you are present at both the Source and the outermost part. Your being is not separate from God. So, although you "ride" the current of sound, you really are not going anywhere, except more fully into your awareness of yourself and your own divinity. When I practice the Sound Current, as the form which holds the Traveler Consciousness, I don't go anywhere. I am the Sound, so there's nowhere to go. When I work with you as my students and assist you in traveling on the Sound Current, I take you and ride it with you so you will gain the sense of movement and progress. Becoming adept at traveling the Sound Current is one way to be everywhere at one time, bring everything to one place, and have universal knowing. There is no separation anywhere in the universes. Everything is God. Everything is one. You need only expand your awareness to include it all.

An initiate of mine once got himself into a situation where it looked as though he was going to be physically beaten up by several men. As they were coming toward him, he envisioned me at my home and inwardly sent me the message, "I need some help." But by this time, the men had gotten to him and started punching. It took a couple of minutes for the spiritual energy to back them off. My friend wasn't seriously hurt, and when he got to a phone, he called me and asked if I could explain what happened and "why it took so long for the Light to work." I said, "You envisioned me at home, and it took me awhile to get from my home to where you were. If you had envisioned me in your heart, it would have been done instantly. It's a good thing I wasn't traveling in Europe, or you might have really been beaten up." He got the idea that I'm present with him all the time, and he doesn't have to go outside of himself to reach me.

When you create a separation and start placing God, the Traveler, or the Light somewhere outside of yourself, you are involved in illusion. When you ask for the Light in the honesty and purity of your heart, it's present before you can even finish asking. It's faster than your thought. Once you are attuned to the Light, you don't even need to ask for it. You need only ask that your eyes be open to see it and your heart be open to receive it. If you are already attuned to the Light, asking for it can become redundant.

As you enter into spiritual studies and start looking at the possibility of initiation, you might ask yourself how to discern a Light consciousness and a path of upliftment from one of illusion and darkness. Is there any way to know? There really isn't, except to check and test *everything* that comes to you. That's probably the most important single thing I can tell you. *Test Spirit constantly.* Even after you've chosen a spiritual path to follow and have become committed to your growth through its particular discipline, keep testing all that is given to you, all that is shown you. *You* are responsible for your own growth and your own progression. No one else is. Ultimately it will just be you with you, and you are responsible for making sure you are taken care of, protected, and safe.

The eleven steps of the upward path are good guidelines. If you are working with a group which expresses those eleven steps and is striving to maintain high levels of integrity, both individually and collectively, you're probably connecting into a Light consciousness and will be in good territory. If you find yourself working with people who are expressing the qualities of the downward path, be careful. You might want to reevaluate the company you are keeping and the direction you are moving.

One reason it is difficult to discern Spirit fully is that there is no way you can understand Spirit (which is infinite) with your mind (which is finite). The mind, emotions, imagination and unconscious are all tools of the lower worlds—tools designed to give you mobility and facility here in these levels. Spirit goes beyond all of that. You have to "catch" it in your heart. If you try to understand it, you'll fail. In the same way, there is no way you can fathom the Traveler consciousness from any level other than the Traveler consciousness. There is no way it can be measured. It's nature is constant movement and stillness. It is on all levels and moving through them continually. And it's completely stationary because there is nowhere to go.

Your experience is your best indicator of whether or not a particular spiritual path has validity for you. Many years ago I was traveling in India with my staff, and we were told of a yogi in the south of India who was reputed to be the "most highly developed yogi in all of India." So we decided to go and visit this man. We were part of a small gathering who were there that day. We were taken into a room, and the yogi came in and sat with us. We were told we would meditate with the Master for an hour. At the end of the hour, we found out we had been "initiated" into yani yoga. I had not experienced any great change in myself, but I didn't discount the possibility that something very subtle had happened. So I checked it out for a time but didn't discern any greater upliftment in my life. From any point of view, the "initiation" was ineffectual.

Be careful about becoming involved with a spiritual Master who "initiates" you right away. Initiation is not to be entered into without consideration and understanding. It is not a path of the emotions or the mind. It is a path of love and devotion, and it takes time and experience to evolve honestly to a place of love, devotion and *trust* within your inner consciousness. It's not a process to be rushed. That's why I require a minimum of two years study in MSIA before I consider initiating someone. Two years gives you time to come and observe, to test me, measure me, doubt me, look around at the other people who are involved, check things out, and see if you find this way to be valid for you. There's no rush. I also get a chance to observe you, to see if you can maintain a positive focus, if you will make positive choices in your life, and if you behave in ways that are uplifting to yourself and others around you. There is a lot of leeway on this path, and there is great understanding of all the foibles of the human nature, but there is also a commitment to the upward path of Spirit that will not be compromised. After two years, if a student wishes to be initiated and has demonstrated that he can hold the positive commitment to himself and to Spirit, it's karmically clear. Then the work begins in earnest.

I've had students come up to me after studying discourses and coming to seminars for three or four years and say, "What's this thing about initiation?" I say, "Yes, you are eligible to apply for initiation after two years of study." They say, "Well, I've been studying for four years; why didn't you tell me?" I say, "It's a *minimum* of two years. And in the meantime, you have to wake up enough to ask me. That you didn't know enough to ask me is indicative that you weren't quite ready." If someone studies for three or four years before asking for initiation, there is no delay. There has been nothing denied or held back. All things are perfect in their unfoldment. The Traveler is working in Spirit with people who will not know that consciousness in a physical form for ten, fifteen, maybe twenty years. That is not a delay. They are not being left out. When they *do* come into the physical presence of the Traveler, their progression and growth will accelerate rapidly. They'll come into MSIA, and in a few short months will appear to have outstripped the student who has been here for years and years. The physical appearance of "progress" is very tricky and often misleading. The inner experience is the only level you can trust.

In the two years of preparation for initiation, I assist you in building the strength within you necessary for your greater freedom. But it's possible to be free inside of yourself without knowing how to get outside of yourself into the liberation of Spirit. Once you've gained freedom within you, it's very easy to give you spiritual liberation. That's my job and my pleasure.

Perhaps you have been initiated by another spiritual teacher who works through another line of discipline. You might ask, "What happens with that initiation? Am I bound by it?" Yes, you are. Initiations are very powerful, especially if you have been initiated into a specific line of energy and spiritual authority. Perhaps you now decide you want to be initiated by the Traveler, in the line of energy that comes forward through the Movement of Spiritual Inner Awareness. That's possible. It will be necessary for you to responsibly finish your inner work and commitment to the other initiation, and that can be accomplished in many, many individual ways. There is nothing to be concerned about. If you are an initiate of another Master, it is part of your experience and discipline to complete that action. Perhaps you need the discipline as it is brought forward on that path. Whatever your experience is, it is bringing you growth, progression and upliftment. There is nothing "wrong" in God's universes. There is absolutely nothing wrong. So be thankful for your experience, whatever it may be.

If you have taken the "initiation" of drugs or liquor or other obviously negative "masters," you may want to make some other choices in your life. Those things are not loving masters, although they can, indeed, master you and place you in bondage. There is seldom any love in those expressions. If there is not love on your path, change it. Love—loving—is the single most important quality in this world. I'm not talking about sex, controlling "love," or relationships born out of lack and need. I'm talking about the sustaining energy that is of God. That's love. If you don't have love as your reference point, you'll never know when you have found the heart of God, because you won't have an indicator inside of you for that experience. Love knows love because it reflects itself. When you develop within yourself the quality and "fabric" of loving, you will know loving when it presents itself to you from outside. If you do not have a reference point for loving inside yourself, you will not know when love is presented to you.

If you feel you do not experience the quality of loving inside of yourself, do whatever you need to do to get that experience. Put yourself around people who are loving. Watch how they behave. Get professional help if necessary. Do spiritual exercises. Meditate. Get into an area of service where you can express love.

You might want to visit hospitals, read to older people who can no longer do that for themselves, work with children who need someone to love and take care of them, or run errands for someone who cannot get out of the house. Express yourself in loving ways, and that quality will grow and expand and become more evident within you. Love attracts love. The more love you give, the more you receive. It works the other way, too. The more you abuse and hurt people, the more you receive that expression from others. If you are producing pain in others, you will get pain. One day you'll say, "Hey, I've learned that lesson. I don't need to do that anymore." Then you'll change and start producing love.

When you awaken to the love present for you in Spirit, you can start transforming your life. When you are awake and attuned to the love which is present, it makes it very easy for the Traveler to come in and work with you, because love is the Traveler's nature. Love is the Soul's nature. Love is what we're all about. When you awaken to the consciousness of the Traveler inside of you, that consciousness goes with you as you start down the path of life. It goes with you when you go to bed; it gets up with you in the morning. It's with you as you interact with people. It smooths out the bumps in the road and lifts you over the rough spots. Some people will see the Traveler's presence as a purple flash on the periphery of their vision. It's subtle. You might see it flash ahead of you on the road as you're driving. You might see it as you wake up in the morning and open your eyes for the first time. You might see it on your hand as you make a gesture, or around someone's head as you're talking to them.

When the Traveler calls your name, whether you're awake or asleep, the energy of Spirit goes into the center of your being. And in its own time, it starts growing. It grows exactly and precisely the way you'd want it to grow if you could set it up in your wildest imagination. But in your wildest imagination you might forget the reality of it and how to maintain it all the time. What would your wildest imagination be? Let's say it would be *joy*. In your wildest imagination, imagine *joy*. How can you create joy? Can you create joy by doing bad things? I doubt it. The way to have joy is to do good things, joyful things, things that are fun and bring happiness to everyone around you. Do joyful things and you get joy immediately. Do you have joy and laughter when you're frowning and crying? Hardly! Laugh and you generate more laughter. Laugh and the world suddenly becomes sunny and warm and loving and fun. *Those* are the qualities you're after!

If you are going to grow and progress in Spirit, you need joy, love, and the Light and Sound of God. Why? Those qualities will give you the strength to continually reach upward. The Sound will be your guide to follow. The Light will assist you to see where you're going so you do not stumble and fall. The love will give you the endurance to keep going. Love, Light, and Sound—the trinity. Those qualities are present in everyone, even in people who are seemingly not expressing them. They've just got them put away under lock and key somewhere. Someday they'll find the key or discover the combination that will unlock them. Maybe they failed the memory course. What happens spiritually if they don't change their expression and continue with their negativity? When they leave the body at the time of death, the lock is blasted open, and they start all over again. The process of blasting open the lock has traditionally been called purgatory, punishment, or hell. It's not necessarily a negative process. It is one of purification, awareness and growth. It may not be the nicest way to grow, but it's effective. Actually, some people have expressed such negativity in their lives that the process of "purgatory" seems like heaven, while people who are more highly evolved would look upon it as hell. It depends on your perspective.

A *lot* can depend on perspective. When some people meet me, they say, "Oh, yes, he's a spiritual man. He's very loving in his approach to people." Other people look at me and say, "He's full of deceit, greed, and lust. He's a fraud." What's happening? When people see me, they see a mirror. So what they see depends on themselves. The Traveler consciousness acts as a reflector. You see precisely what you put in front of it. But however you relate to me on the physical level, the consciousness of the Traveler always channels energy into your Soul. I am always building the God form in you, assisting you to awaken to the God within, to your own spiritual form. I don't care how you perceive me; the work I do is independent of those levels. Someone can perceive me in a very negative way and still receive an awakening of Spirit inside of them and be charged to go out and do Spirit's work—without ever being consciously aware of the process until much later.

If you decide to work toward initiation, the first two years will be a time of continually taking of the Light and Spirit around you. That's the way you grow; it's expected. There is a lot of work to be done. There is

30

a lot of past karma to be balanced, cleared and released. It's not unusual for some very strange things to
happen in your life. Old situations you thought were
behind you may suddenly reappear, and you have the
chance to balance them and bring love into them.
Things you handled badly in your life may present
themselves to you again—and you have the chance to
do better. It's important to use every opportunity to
balance things. What doesn't get worked out physically
may be able to be cleared in the "night travel." The
Mystical Traveler has the ability to work with you in the
subtle levels of your consciousness while your physical
body is sleeping. The Traveler can assist you to work
out your karma through your dreams. Sometimes the
karma can be dissolved in these subtle levels so that it's
unnecessary to work it out physically. This is the grace
which the Traveler can extend to you.

Sometimes when you are working out a karmic
situation in the night travel, you wake up and feel like
you're running a fever. You might wonder if you're
coming down with the flu or some sickness. It may be
that the seeds of karma are actually being burned out
of you. Within a few minutes, you'll usually feel fine,
and you'll wonder what is happening. Spiritually, this
purification process is like taking a laser beam of Light
and burning out the "seeds" that have held your
negativity and karma. If this kind of thing happens, just
let it be. You don't have to be concerned or frightened.
Just place yourself in the Light and ask for the Light to
fill, surround and protect you. You might want to keep
a glass of water by your bed to drink as you release the
situation into God's hands.

As you become more aware of your multidimensional nature, you become more adept at shifting from one level to another. The most beautiful and profound things can be happening on the spiritual levels, and you can go right on with the "ordinariness" of your physical life. Great realizations can come to you while showering or mowing the lawn. One level does not negate the other. All levels exist simultaneously. You can learn to flow smoothly between them all.

As you move into initiation, you can look for four inward signs of initiation. First, at the time of the first physical initiation when you receive a tone connecting you to the Sound Current, the form of the Mystical Traveler in the causal level awakens itself inside you and gives you constant guidance from that day forward. It doesn't give you constant information. You can't ask it "twenty questions"—or four hundred questions! It gives you the guidance of Spirit within you.

The form of the Traveler has always been present within you but becomes energized at the time of initiation. That's the good news and the bad news. The good news is that it's there. The bad news is that you've never realized it before. You ask, "How could it always have been there without my ever knowing it?" You've been focused on other things, and you don't always focus on the things that are most valuable to you. Have you ever been driving down the road and made the wrong turn off the highway because you were daydreaming or thinking about something other than your destination? Sure, even though you would probably say it's valuable for you to pay attention to where you're going. But you didn't do it. Guess what? That's being very human. It's not wrong. It's not bad. It's just the way it is.

32

You don't have to feel badly that you didn't discover your spiritual path two years ago or twenty years ago. You don't have to be upset with yourself that you are not fully awakened to the Spirit within you. You can be upset if you want, but it won't serve to awaken you to Spirit any faster. So you can just let it go and love yourself. God won't punish you. Why should he when his work is to awaken you inside? God is not in the business of punishment; God is in the business of upliftment. When you stop beating yourself up for all your various "sins" and just open yourself up to the presence of the Lord, you'll find yourself beginning to lift in consciousness automatically. That's a joyful day.

The second inward sign of initiation is that the Traveler in a radiant form is able to take the initiate anywhere in the spiritual worlds. When you get above the causal realm and begin reaching into the mental and etheric realms, the Traveler may appear in *any form*. When you reach Soul initiation, you'll again see the Traveler in the radiant form. In the lower realms, the form of the Traveler might look like my physical form. Or it might look like a flash of purple or another form entirely. You may recognize it; you may not. Usually if you look at the eyes, you will know the Traveler by the love present. The Traveler will appear to you from the right side or from straight ahead of you. If the form appears from the left side, it is probably the Kal or negative power. Can you be tricked by an illusionary form? Yes. How can you guard against the illusion? Use your initiatory tone inwardly. Chant silently and if the form is not the Traveler it will move away. The Mystical Traveler is a permanent consciousness which stays with the initiate.

If you wish to exemplify the consciousness of an initiate, keep your attitude positive. It's very true that you can learn and grow through negative situations, but it is also very true that if you are smart, you can learn and grow faster through positive experiences and situations. You do not have to berate yourself to learn. If you make a mistake, turn it to your advantage. Learn the lesson and move on. Don't prove your growth by negativity. Prove it by positiveness so you'll have joy on your side as well as everything else.

Spirit's lessons are continuous. They come through many forms and situations. Watch for the one who comes to you as your teacher. Your spouse might be your teacher one day, your employer the next, and your son or daughter the next. The Traveler will bring your lessons to you in any way that will be effective. When you maintain an open attitude, you will learn the lessons much faster. If you limit the recognition of your teachers to only a few, you limit your learning. Everyone who comes to you may be your teacher. Be open and be the best student you can. You'll move ahead faster.

The third inward sign of initiation becomes apparent at the time the physical body undergoes death. Then the Traveler defeats the Angel of Death and places the initiate in the best spiritual region for his greater spiritual growth. Other people at the time of death are turned over to the negative power which "chews" on the Soul. It's been called the death of a thousand scorpion stings. It's considered painful. Experiencing that process once is enough to make you resolve to find another way, which is why some of you have found this path of initiation to the Sound Current.

The Angel of Death is actually defeated at the time of initiation because the Sound of God is placed in the initiate as an awakening consciousness. The devil form, the Angel of Death, cannot approach and must stand aside. It may come up to you and try to distract you or have you turn from the spiritual form and give it up. It can play all sorts of tricks, but it cannot touch you. All you have to do is stand strong and say, "Get thou behind me, Satan." You don't even have to say that. There's an old Irish saying, "May you be in heaven half an hour before the devil knows you're dead." When you are an initiate of the Traveler, you *are* in heaven before the devil knows you're dead. It's an easy process.

The fourth inward sign of initiation is that an initiate who has loyally carried out his devotion is permanently free from cycles of birth and death. He does not have to be born again, in any sense. Even though the initiate who has neglected his devotional practices and spiritual exercises may be brought back into the physical body again, he is placed in circumstances where devotion to the Lord is the central theme of his life. He is given a better than even break in his next incarnation. Perhaps he'll be born into a family of all initiates to the Sound Current and grow up with complete devotion to this path. It will just be a time to complete and bring together the loose ends, and he will break free of the incarnation patterns in that next life.

Many of the youngsters who are being born to those who are my initiates now are completing their last lifetime here. They are being given great blessings and a chance to increase their devotional consciousness. When they grow up, there will be a great joy with them that would be very hard to understand if you did not know what was happening.

Because so many Souls are coming into the world now from very high levels of spiritual consciousness, there is a great responsibility being placed on parents today. For a long time there were a lot of astral entities coming into the earth plane who would choose any vehicle through which to embody. During that time, abortions became very common. Spiritually there was little karma attached to having an abortion at that time, as it was not affecting the spiritual levels to any great degree. That time is ending. The new age is so close that angels of God's Light are now coming into physical embodiment, and we have tremendous responsibility to these children. If you have conceived and the child you carry is a master's Soul coming here to complete its physical experiences or to bring uplift-ment to mankind, it may not be spiritually clear to abort that child.

You may have to be very careful in your sexual recreation, because if you do not abstain and become pregnant, you may be responsible for bringing a Soul into the world. This is serious. Mothers who are not in marriage patterns can still have the child and raise it in a spiritual community, according to the word of God and with the love and support present in the spiritual family. However, the responsibility is to become so devoted to your spiritual practices that you do not enter into the lusts of life and let them control you.

There are always prerequisites to becoming an in-itiate. Initiates must be earning an honest living and sharing it with those to whom they have responsibility. Honestly dealing in your labors of life means you don't hurt yourself and don't hurt others. You take care of yourself so you can help take care of others. You must be paid for the labor of your life, and it must be shared with those who are needy and those who are building a group consciousness and sense of community. Married couples share in this responsibility. So if the man works and the woman cares for the home and children and supports her husband in loving consciousness, she is also working. And if the woman works and the man cares for the home and supports her, he is also working. When you are married, this is a shared action. The responsibility is to build for those who come behind us so they may have greater advantage over the negative power.

The negative power is becoming stronger on the planet. The stronger it gets, the more the Holy Spirit will pour its energy forth into the hearts of men. We're going to see more demonstrations of negativity on this planet, and at the same time, we're going to see greater manifestations of God's presence through the Spirit than have been seen in the last two thousand years, and maybe in the last twenty-five thousand years.

As you take initiation and move into the spiritual levels, you take the opportunity to become a positive focus and force upon this earth. The more energy you place into the spiritual levels through your spiritual exercises, the more you can increase your awareness of the higher levels. As you learn to lift in your consciousness, you can get a more realistic perspective on the physical level. Instead of thinking the physical level is all-important, you start to see it as only a part of the whole, and not a very big part, at that. Sometimes the energy of Spirit floods through you so powerfully that you feel absolutely "charged" with energy. Your body might feel "nervous" because of all the energy. Your mind may start racing with all sorts of creative thoughts. When that happens, start *moving* on the ideas. Start moving with the energy. If you don't, it will start settling into the emotions, and you interrupt Spirit's process by interpreting it emotionally and becoming fearful or neurotic. You can frighten and disturb yourself if you don't *use* the energy.

Take care of this physical level. It's important. You create your habits here. You serve yourself well if you create good habits. My mother used to get after me to make my bed every morning, and I couldn't understand why because every night it would become unmade again. In her own way she explained that making the bed, cleaning my room, showering, brushing my teeth—all those mundane levels of liv-ing—were part of demonstrating respect and love for the God that dwells within me. We each are a part of God, very specifically and literally. We honor the God within by doing good things both in this world and in the higher worlds.

You cannot neglect this level and call yourself spiritual. If you want to be eccentric and get away with it, it's also important to maintain a certain amount of practicality. If you have your life together, have a good family life, are holding a good job, making good money and paying your bills, you can rant and rave and roll around on your living room floor, and everybody says, "Yeah, but everything else in his life is fine, so it must be okay." If you're an undependable "slob" who borrows money from everyone around and acts weird, they lock you up. If you want to be eccentric (which can sometimes be another word for free), get your life together. Then you can do some eccentric things if you want.

Maintain the mundane levels. That may come down to simply breathing in and out when the going gets rough. Breathing is the simplest meditation. When life starts falling apart all around you and you don't even have time to call in the Light, just take a deep breath. Breathe in the positive and breathe out the negative. If your emotions are kicking up on you, just take in a deep breath, gather your emotions up into that breath, and then release them as you breathe out. And if you need to, do it again and again.

You have dominion over yourself and your expression. Ask for the Light to be with you. Focus on the Light. Recognize yourself as a child of God who deserves all that is good. As you hold that focus inside of yourself, you'll create it. You can create good feelings, happiness, joy, and a quality of peace within you. When you start to experience bliss, you know you have tapped into the Soul level energy. When that starts to happen, you'll know who to take your initiation from. When you start to experience the loving inside, you'll know your path. There will be no way to deny it. When you realize you hardly notice what used to drive you into negativity, you'll start to know the value of the spiritual path and recognize initiation as an integral part of it.

Initiation awakens you to the spiritual levels on which you already live. You have your physical home on this level, a home for your imagination on the astral level, and a home for your emotions on the causal level. Your mind lives in the mental realm, and the unconscious resides in the etheric realm. Although you live in all those realms simultaneously, you have so focused your awareness in these lower levels and all their folderol that you do not pay attention to the higher levels. For all you know, you might be a king or queen on a higher level of Spirit. If that be so, what are you doing living here in poverty? Suppose you're a god on another realm. You denigrate that position by living here in emotional turmoil and anxiety. Is it possible? Yes, it's not only possible, it's a reality. When will you realize it? I can't answer that for you. You have to decide. Will you awaken to your divinity? Yes, ultimately. What does that mean? It means it could be a long time. But in Spirit all time is now, so in a sense it doesn't matter. It matters only in the sense that it is quite wonderful to have those greater realizations of Spirit and the awareness of the God within. And since you will awaken to that ultimately, why not do it now?

I talk about the Spirit and tell you of the God within and the higher realms of Spirit as a means of awakening you to those greater levels. You might say, "What good does it do to hear your words if I don't know them for myself?" If I didn't keep putting out the message, you might not turn in this direction for a long, long time. You might become so caught up in the illusions of the world you wouldn't look toward Spirit for eons. I love you and want to share the joy of Spirit with you. You can learn through joy. You can learn through upliftment. You can also learn through pain and anguish, but why make those choices if you have others? Pain is not a negative process; it lets you know you're awake and alive. Pain can be a strengthener. Grief can be a strengthener. Feelings of intimidation, worry, fear, confusion—they're all potential strengtheners. Don't curse those things that appear negative. You can use them as a springboard to lift you into Spirit and to build strength.

Suppose you have a piece of gold which you want to make into a beautiful chalice, but you don't know how to do that. So you take it to a goldsmith who has the skill to make the chalice. You give him the gold and you release it. You don't care if he melts it, hammers it, molds it, shapes it, or even throws away the parts that contain impurities as he makes it into a beautiful chalice. You don't care about the process of transformation as it goes from a rough piece of gold to the golden chalice. The result is worth it. The beauty of the final product is worth everything that has been part of the process.

When you move toward God consciousness, you give your consciousness over to God and ask him to make you into the golden chalice. God will do it precisely the way that is perfect for you. What do you care if you have an ache or a pain along the way? What does it matter if you're a little depressed one day or a little confused another? If I work with you as one of my students to prepare you for initiation, there are often areas that need to be rearranged. If you were already perfect, you would have already reached God realization. You must bring yourself into line with spiritual direction. When things disturb you, move to the higher perspective and see where it might fit in the larger picture. *If you complain about the work that Spirit does with you, Spirit backs off.* Then you complain because nothing is going on! Don't complain, because God is molding you into the golden chalice and is separating out the impurities from the gold. When the chalice is completed, the Traveler will come along and give you jewels to add to it and enhance its beauty.

You are loved. You are protected. Nothing is going to happen to you that is not for your upliftment. When you become an initiate of the Traveler, the Traveler becomes devoted to you in a very specific and literal sense. The Traveler does not forget you, even when you forget him. When you don't meditate, the Traveler meditates for you. When you don't do your job, the Traveler does it for you. You won't progress too rapidly this way, because I have a lot of initiates, and it takes time for me to get around to everyone. You'll move a lot faster if you hold up your end and do the work that is yours to do in a loving and joyful way.

You can build strength through every situation that appears to you. If someone comes up to you with some marijuana and wants you to join him in smoking it, you can go with him, roll it, get it all ready, and then put it down and walk out. You'll build strength. You can go to your cupboard and take out the liquor bottle and pour the booze down the sink without taking that final drink. If you're overweight, you can cook a beautiful steak and throw it in the garbage disposal. Or you can go into a restaurant and order a wonderful meal but not eat it. Yes, I agree, it's a crazy point of view, but watch the strength you'll build. You build integrity. You build character. You build your own trust in yourself as you learn to keep your word and be true to yourself. Integrity is an indicator in the physical world of spirituality.

Your word should be like the North Star which remains constant. Once you have given your word in a sincere or spiritual way, it should remain constant. If you change it, you are not really following a path of upliftment. You're following a path of manipulation, attempting to manipulate people in their relationships to you. Usually your attempts to manipulate are based upon your emotions, your thoughts, or your imagination which create all sorts of illusion and delusion.

Take the time in your life to consider your path. Make your choices based upon the best and most accurate information available to you. Don't rush into changes. Meditate upon your life's path. Ask for Spirit's guidance. If you are involved in something you would like to change, ask for Spirit or the Traveler to take the old pattern from you, and then let it go. It sounds simple, and it is. It is not necessarily easy. When you are willing to let go of those things which have not worked for you in your life, ask the Traveler to take them. And then just move on to another expression in your life, not looking back or being concerned about "what happened." Be willing to move forward on your path.

Be willing to drop the criteria of the physical, mental, emotional and financial levels and move to the spiritual. Be willing to sacrifice the lower levels to gain the Spirit. If you want to travel the path of the Sound Current initiations of the Traveler, you must be willing to reach beyond the limitations of the material worlds in order to gain the awareness of your life in the spiritual worlds.

3
Recognizing Mastership

It is through loving made manifest that you are able to recognize a Master. Love is the greatest step of mastership. When loving is expressed, all other aspects of mastership fall into place and blend into the loving. It is the greatest of the keys.

There have been many masters who have walked the face of the earth and shared their awareness of Spirit and God with those who were not yet awakened. The office of the Christ has forever been the Logos of this particular planet on which we dwell. Many have fulfilled that office. There is always at least one on the planet who manifests the Christ in physical consciousness. There is a new dispensation of Spirit which has moved upon us in recent times and brings the timeless knowledge that the Christ has never left the planet. In this sense, it becomes foolish to wait for His return. The spiritual being you have been waiting for is already here and has been here for a long time. You can evoke the spiritual form of the Christ within your consciousness. It's easy because you are a child of God, as we are all children of God. You are heir to divinity. It is your birthright.

Jesus filled the office of the Christ for a time and represented one of its highest manifestations. For this alone we call Him the elder brother. He took the consciousness of the Christ, lifted, demonstrated, and exemplified it, then gave it to all of us. He, more than anyone who had gone before Him, stated that the heritage of the Christ consciousness belonged to all. Through the line of the Christ we all become one body dwelling in God consciousness. We all become the Christ dwelling within Christ consciousness. The Mystical Traveler line comes down through the center of the Christ consciousness into this planet. In other planets it doesn't come through the Christ. It comes through the All in the All or the It of Itself.

Historically there have been many throughout the ages who have been in the line of the Traveler's energy and brought the message of Spirit to humanity. At different times in history, the priorities of mankind have varied, and the Traveler adapts Spirit's message to match the shifting priorities while maintaining the inherent integrity of the message.

When the ideal of sacrifice was highly esteemed by the people, Abraham gave his message. Some things must always be sacrificed to gain the next level. When beauty was worshipped beyond all else, Joseph, the handsome one, gave the message of Spirit. His message was the beauty of the earth and the beauty of his own beingness, which stood as an example to all. The beauty and the love of his heart touched all whom he saved from famine in Egypt, as well as his brothers and father.

When people became curious about miracles, Moses brought forward his message and performed miracles for the people. Moses was in the line of Christ and the Travelers, the line of authority that goes back to the beginning of time and beyond time into the heart of God.

When music was regarded as celestial and a conveyance for the Word of God, David gave the message of Spirit in song and created "songs of praise and thanksgiving unto God." (Nehemiah 13:36) When Solomon delivered his message, wealth was greatly prized and esteemed. So he presented the idea of Spirit in terms of wealth and wisdom. When the two harlots came before him with a child they each claimed as their own, King Solomon listened to their claims and said, " 'Bring me a sword. Divide the living child in two and give half to the one and half to the other.' Then spake the woman whose the living child was unto the king....and she said, 'O my lord, give *her* the living child and in no wise slay it.' " (I Kings 3:24, 25, 26) Solomon recognized the *wealth* of loving compassion the mother had for her child and knew her to be the true mother. He said, " 'Give her the living child and in no wise slay it; she is the mother therof.' And all Israel heard of the judgment which the king had judged; and they feared the king: for they saw that the wisdom of God was in him to do judgment." (I Kings 3:27, 28) King Solomon brought forward the message of wealth—not just material wealth, but wealth of Spirit and wisdom.

At the time when heredity was recognized, Jesus gave Spirit's message as the Son of God. Some people have said Jesus was the Prince of Peace, but He did not proclaim Himself as that. He proclaimed Himself as the Son of God. When the concept of democracy was prevalent, Mohammed gave the message that God is like all and God is among all. He proclaimed, "There is no God but God." Bahaullah came forward and gave his message as the Prince of Peace.

Each Traveler has given the message of his time. All the messages are as relevant and applicable today as they were then. You need only attune yourself to the spiritual message beyond their words and apply it to your present-day reality. The good works of all the Travelers are brought forward to this time, now. Those of us who stand in the line of the Traveler reap the reward and become the chosen people of this day. I'm not talking about "chosen people" in a religious sense, but in the sense that those who choose God and choose to follow Spirit in their lives are, in return, chosen by Spirit. Spirit chooses *everyone*; when you choose back you awaken to the fact that you are one of the chosen.

God constitutes all beingness, both individually and collectively. Every Soul has the source of the divine message within itself. The part of you which is the Christ has Christ's message. That part of you that is the Traveler has the Traveler's message. The message of Spirit resides in Spirit; that's where it will always be. You cannot be taught the message of God; you *awaken* to it. When someone who is awake in Spirit speaks from that source, the corresponding part of you stirs in recognition and begins to awaken. If the Christ

47

were to come again in a physical body to the planet, you would only know Him as the Christ in you recognized Him.

The Christ, as I speak of it, is a universal consciousness. The consciousness of the Traveler is universal, not bound or limited by culture or tradition. The Traveler is as present in Eastern tradition as Western. It's as present in other universes as it is here. There are no boundaries of space and time. There are no limitations of society. The consciousness of the Traveler is free.

In this time, the Traveler has come forward and identified himself openly. The Preceptor consciousness is also present and says to you, "The promises have been given for many eons of time. The promises are fulfilled." The prophet Joel prophesied, "And it shall come to pass in the last days, saith God, I will pour out of my Spirit upon all flesh." (Acts 2:17) "And it shall come to pass that whosoever shall call on the name of the Lord shall be saved." (Acts 2:21) That is the message now, of this age. The heritage of God is waiting to be claimed. You can partake of God. You need not define God or make yourself right or others wrong. You can just be one with God and live from your loving heart.

People say, "If I could just become one with God, if I could have a sign from heaven, I would be happy." Where do you think you came from? You *are* of God. God is your source. There is no part which is not of God. You don't need definitions in this new age. You need the love of the spiritual heart. God's love is manifest within you. You would not be living were it not for God's love. It is your matrix. You can express God's loving through all levels of your beingness. Love is of the spiritual heart. Love is also of the mind, emotions, and body. Love is of God. As you reach into your heart and manifest love, you have fulfilled all the laws and prophecies. You manifest your divinity for all to see. You do not have to parade your divinity by putting yourself up or others down because everyone shares equally in God's Spirit.

Let loving express God's presence in all that you do. When you speak, speak with love. When you think, think loving thoughts. When you act, act in love. When you use your ego as a thrust into this world, use it in the name of love, so that your works are good and bring goodness to everyone around you. Love is love by itself, but it can use everything to express into the world. When you do not express lovingly, you do not truly live. When you do not live, God cannot pour forth his energies into the world through you.

Beyond the ability to recognize a Master consciousness, I have been asked how it is possible to know a Spiritual Traveler or Mystical Traveler—one who cannot only awaken you to mastership but can assist you in gaining Soul transcendence. You can recognize a Master by looking for the eleven steps to mastership. But there are also twelve specific signs by which you can recognize a Traveler.

First, the Traveler lives as an ordinary citizen. He could be married, single, divorced, or living with someone outside of marriage. Any "lifestyle" of an ordinary man might also be that of the Traveler. He lives an ordinary life—not a high life or a low life. Ordinariness is the condition just prior to God. When you become ordinary and cease to look upon yourself as unique or separate, you flow with the Spirit as it is present and become one with it and thus with God.

The second sign of a Traveler is that he does nothing to distinguish himself from the people among whom he lives. Some spiritual teachers and masters set themselves apart from their students by wearing specially colored robes, turbans, or other ornaments and paraphernalia. That is a little like moving into a community with all the people you love and then putting a fortress around your house so you can be uniquely separate from the people you love and want to be with. It doesn't make a lot of sense. If you set up your flag of separateness, you become a leader of flagpoles, not a lover among people. There are reasonable times when leaders must be separate from others, just as there are reasonable times when everyone must be separate from others. There are reasonable times in your life when you must take time for yourself, away from the distractions of others—time to pray, meditate, rest, and revitalize yourself. That's not what I'm talking about. I'm talking about the attitude of, "I'm special and unique and greater than you." *That* kind of separateness is not a part of the Traveler's expression.

The third sign of a Traveler is that he has never separated his initiates or set one part of the group apart from another or allowed a caste system to evolve. He may delineate what is already present—like saying, "She is on that chair, and he is on the chair over there." That is just identifying choices which have already been made; it is not *making* those choices. The

Traveler will never divide his people by encouraging separate dress, headgear, housing, ornaments, or other methods of separation. The Traveler encourages the experience of oneness in all ways.

The fourth sign of a Traveler is that he does not hide himself in a jungle, on a mountain, or in a cave. Could one who has separated himself and meditated in a remote area for many years become a Traveler later? Sure, if he comes out of the cave and comes down to do "battle" for the Souls of people, to share his love, and to put himself on the line for the salvation of their Souls. The "battleground" for the Soul is where the negative power is most present, and that is in the fields of emotional desire, mental decision, and financial gain. In those levels the negative power sits on the throne. The Traveler comes right into that field of endeavor to demonstrate how the positive power can prevail in the very midst of negativity.

The fifth sign of a Traveler is that he is not interested in founding religions or organizing sects. His work with people cuts across all of humanity regardless of race, creed, color, situation, circumstance or environment. His work encompasses all mankind.

The sixth sign of a Traveler is that he does not promise worldly wealth or success. I don't know how many times I've told people, "I don't promise you anything in the physical world, and when it comes to the spiritual world, there is no need to promise because that is being fulfilled all the time." Promising the spiritual world to you is like promising that you can breathe. It is happening. It is ongoing. You are participating in it right now. There is no need to promise what is already present.

Some people attempt to manipulate Spirit into bringing them wealth or power in worldly manifestation. They go to psychics, use ouija boards, or ask questions of pendulums in an attempt to "get an edge" on life's game. Sometimes they attempt to channel ascended masters, asking for information. The trouble is that the ascended master isn't there to say if the information is right or wrong, so the person gets to manipulate the information and thus manipulate other people who are depending on the information. And if they start to channel contradictory information from the master, there is additional confusion. Inner guidance given by the Traveler will never contradict the outer teachings of the Traveler. There is a oneness of the inner and outer Traveler which precludes contradiction.

Some people attempt to manipulate the world around them by the procurement of spiritual charms, amulets, medallions, and so forth. The Traveler will never give any such device as a means to gain worldly success. Things like crosses, stars of David, Hu pendants, pins, and crystal hearts can all be used to reflect back to you the nature of God. Thus, such reminders can have value for you as you use them in a valuable way. They are not magnetized or charged to be used for any type of control, travel, divination or anything paranormal.

The seventh sign of a Traveler is that he does not recall dead spirits or practice any form of occultism. Calling of dead spirits might look like entering into a trance state and calling upon a spirit to speak through you. The Traveler does not practice this type of thing. The Traveler is aware that when a Soul departs from this physical world, its experience here is over, and it has gone to another place to continue its experience on another level. To attempt to bring a Soul back to this level can cause delay spiritually. It is not a loving action or one that is spiritually clear.

The eighth sign of a Traveler is that he is spiritually perfect and can extend spiritual perfection to his initiates by connecting them to the Word of God, which purifies and brings perfection to them. This is not done in the physical level because nothing can be perfect on this physical level except change. The Word of God produces a change perfectly, which is reflected inwardly on the spiritual form, not outwardly on the physical form that is gathered around the spiritual form. The physical form will never be perfect, and because it is not perfect, it is always in a state of change. As soon as you are born, you have the disease of death already in you. By your birth into the physical world, you have set your limitations and have contracted for the end of this form. That which is perfect, Spirit and Soul, does not end with physical death. The perfection is infinite. The imperfect baggage connected to Soul undergoes the process of purification through initiation into the Sound Current. It's not unlike getting the pearl out of a clam. You just have to open it up, reach in there and take the pearl. It is that "pearl of great price" with which we deal. I hear theologians sometimes refer to the Soul as "crippled." That's just nonsense. There is no Soul that is crippled. All Souls are perfect. Anyone who says otherwise hasn't seen the Soul.

The ninth sign of a Traveler is that he comes as a giver, not a receiver. He gives the very essence of life. He gives encouragement and support. He gives the seed of awakening faith and hope, but at the same time he gives these qualities, he destroys them because the experience of reality is the foundation you must stand upon. If you stand on any other quality, you'll fall. If you only have hope and faith without reality, at some point you become discouraged and say, "Where am I going with all this faith and hope? What is it doing for me?" It's like someone continually telling you the check is in the mail, but it never gets to you. You have faith and hope that you'll receive it, but you never do. At some point, you start wondering what's going on. When you get in the car, drive to the person's house, pick up the check, drive to the bank and deposit the check—*then* you have the reality of the experience.

The tenth sign of a Traveler is that he comes to dispel superstition. I dispel a lot of superstitions by ridicule. People tell me what they are doing and I'll say, "Why on earth would you do that?" They say, "Because I'm hoping *this* will take place." I say, "You mean you're going down track A hoping that you're going to get to track L? Are you hoping two parallel tracks will intersect each other? They don't! You know they don't. What you are promoting is superstition." If you have two events that *are* connected and you change one to affect the other, that can be a valid approach. If you have two events that are *not* connected and you change one in the hopes of affecting the other, you're in trouble.

I used to play basketball with a friend of mine, and this fellow was better than I, but he was superstitious. He "had" to stand in a certain place on the court in order to "make" the shot. So it was easy to guard him. If I could make him move off his "spot," even by inches, I could throw his game off. He had another superstition, which was that he had to dribble twice before he shot. So all I had to do was count; he'd dribble once and I'd hit the ball out of his hands.

I told him how I could read his pattern. He said, "But if I don't dribble twice, it won't go in." And he had set it up so firmly in his consciousness that it appeared to be so. Was it reality or superstition? Definitely superstition. There is no connection between how many times you dribble a ball and how many times you make the shot. They just don't go together. But they did for him.

Eventually, I made his life on the court so miserable that I forced him to learn to vary his game. He *had* to learn to shoot from other places. And he *had* to learn to vary the number of times he dribbled before a shot.

If you have children and you see them starting to create superstitions, talk to them about it. If you let them continue, what starts out as a relatively harmless pattern can become a compulsion that may lead to an obsession. It can lock into the subconscious and unconscious and create a block to spiritual progression. Once those things lock in, they can take a lot of work to change.

The eleventh sign of a Traveler is that he does not perform miracles for public exhibition. He may do so for the spiritual advancement of an initiate. The initiates experience miracles all the time, because they *live* the miracles instead of *looking* for the miracles. Prior to initiation, neophytes may look for the phenomena of miracles and, although I know there are the small daily miracles of perfect timing, I also suggest strongly that they get free of all superstitions and *live* their lives to the fullest. When they do that, their timing automatically becomes perfect. Then they do not have to manipulate their world. They can drive to the store, pull up right in front, and have another car pull out so they can park. It's like someone has been saving a place for them. They don't have to sit and create it in their minds or try to figure some other way to do it; it will just happen. That's the phenomenon of spiritual attunement.

People say God is closer to you than your next breath. Right! He *is* the next breath. And you don't even have to wait for the next one. He is entirely present. God is not solely in the future or solely in the past; God is present. When you live in the moment, you are living in God's timing. If you do mental gymnastics, you are living ahead of yourself, and you'll distort the timing. The timing is a lot better if you just move into the flow of the timing Spirit is already bringing forward for you.

What about planning ahead? You can plan ahead—in the now. How is that done? You cannot be present in the moment and be planning ahead in your mind at exactly the same time because two things cannot occupy the same space and time. But you can change the focus of your attention very rapidly. You can look at one thing, think of something else, hear something else, and keep your attention on all three by moving it from one to the other so rapidly that it looks like a continuum. It's not; those are all separate actions. As you develop your mind, you can keep more things going at what appears to be the same time. There are people who play chess with fifteen or twenty people at the same time. They just walk along making moves, then circle back and keep it all going. But since this is done in the mind, it is not truly a method of planning ahead and being in the now.

Some people have this awareness out of a spiritual form, rather than a mental form. In this way they can plan ahead and still be in the now. These people don't even think. They just become the game. They know the whole process and all the moves before they are even made. But they move through the game in a process of *now*. They do not make a move before its timing, even if they can see it coming. Do you understand that? You never have to do something prior to the moment you have to do it. Sometimes you *think* you do, but you don't. You can always wait until the moment thrusts the action upon you. When the right moment appears, you will not be able to deny the action. Prior to the moment, you may *think* a certain action will be required, but that can always shift before the moment comes present.

The twelfth sign of a Traveler is that he relies solely on the Word of God—not the Word of God as it is printed on a piece of paper or written in a book, but the Word of God as it is given inwardly. The Traveler gives the Word of God to his initiates so they may do likewise. Then we all get to stand in the same line, eat at the same table, and live the same love. There is no more separation, grief, terror or hurt, because we are all together. No man is an island. No man stands alone. Each man's joy is joy to me. And each man's grief my own, although I do not support the expression of grief in my initiates. Grief is nearly always a response based upon a false expectation.

Some people who follow certain religious teachings talk about grief and sorrow experienced relative to the "loss" of Jesus Christ. That's nonsense. Since God and the savior consciousness are truly present, there is no room for sorrow or grief. There is only joy and abundance, no matter what has taken place. The illusion of "loss" holds no power when Spirit is present in your heart. There is always joy in the presence of the Lord. And the presence of the Lord is not a once-in-awhile process. It is a constant, ongoing, moment-to-moment reality.

When you focus on the Lord, you find Him present with you. He has never been apart from you; you have just been distracted by other levels. When you focus on the Lord, you come to know Him. When you know God, you can love God. The keys to the knowledge and love of God are within you. You cannot be taught those things, only awakened to them. When you know God, you will know the Traveler because he comes as an emissary or agent of the Supreme God. There is no separation. The Traveler comes to assist you in awakening *consciously* to the Lord. As you add the strength of consciousness to the intuitive knowledge and love, you can move yourself deeper and higher into awareness of the spiritual realms.

Again, my friends, let me emphasize that you will know the Traveler by the living love that is present for all humanity. Jesus the Christ said it this way, "By this shall all men know that ye are my disciples, if ye have love one to another" (John 14:34). A teacher is one who lives the loving quality. There is only the teacher or wayshower now. You are sophisticated and can go to God directly. God is living love, as *you* must be the same living love to reach him. God is so large that to explore all the levels of God requires such a loving commitment of time that there is no time to pick on people, backbite, or be depressed. You only have time—eternity. All is present inside of you. God has prepared the table of plenty for you. God has placed Souls of resourcefulness here. We are beyond the scriptures. Mohammed completed scripture. Bahaullah completed scripture. All that remains to do is love.

God is dwelling among his chosen people. God is dwelling in the heart. God is greater than the heart. God is all, not a part, yet every part. Love God with all your heart. Love yourself with the same devotion. Love all who come to you as you love God. But practice finding the loving within yourself before you look out. With loving, nothing is impossible. With loving, you can overcome all things. You can overcome your fears, your insecurities, your disturbances, everything. Through the Christ consciousness that is your heritage, you are born anew, resurrected in Spirit.

Buddha said, "I am the Light of Asia." Christ said, "I am the Light of the world." The Traveler says, "I am the Light of the universe." And the Preceptor says, "I am the Light of all universes." This is not a spiritual promise. It is reality. It is present now, as are all the saints and saviors and masters of all time. You breathe the same air that Bahaullah, Mohammed, Jesus, Solomon, David, Moses, Joseph, Abraham, and all the others breathed. When you attune yourself to the Christ, you tune yourself back into the heritage of this whole line of energy and power. Their love and Light comes right down through you, and the only way you can manifest it is to love. Loving is the glory of God made manifest. As you become one in consciousness with this line of spiritual authority, you experience the greatest joy and peace you can ever imagine.

4
The Inner Path
of Mastership

The work the Traveler does with his students and initiates is, for the most part, on the inner levels. It's true that there are also outer teachings in the form of seminars, tapes, books, and discourses. The outer forms are designed to focus and direct the mind and provide a structure to relate to. But the changes, the growth, the learning, and the understanding all take place within you. It is not an outer process as much as an inner one.

The Traveler has the ability to touch the inner consciousness, communicate with you directly through your inner spiritual essence, and affect change from the inside out. Change can never be imposed on you from the outside; change takes place inside first and then manifests on the outer levels.

Spirit resides within. So it stands to reason that spiritual growth and progession happen within. Since the path of initiation is an inward path, you could go through all the levels of initiation and never alter much of your behavior on the outer levels. The Traveler himself operates in the world as an ordinary citizen, yet inwardly holds the keys to a magnificent spiritual consciousness. The Traveler resides inside of you as the Inner Master at the same time he manifests in the world as an outer form. The inner teachings are presented to you continually, twenty-four hours a day, through the presence of the Inner Master.

You may perceive the Inner Master in several ways. You may sense the presence of a magnificence close within you and the protection of love, and you intuitively know you are in communication with that presence and receiving guidance. That's one way to know the Inner Master. You may also see a flash of purple or a flickering of violet or white Light, which may signal the presence of the Inner Master. You might see the eyes of the Inner Master in the inner vision, and they will reflect to you such incredible loving and caring that you feel your "sins," your fears and concerns dissolve in his love. Or you might see, again in the inner vision, the radiant form of the Inner Master, a magnificent form of tremendous beauty and majesty.

In the Book of Revelations in the Bible there is a description of the Inner Master: "I saw seven golden candlesticks; And in the midst of the seven candlesticks one like unto the Son of man, clothed with a garment down to the foot and girt about the paps with a golden girdle. His head and his hairs were white like wool, as white as snow; and his eyes were as a flame of fire; and his feet like unto fine brass, as if they burned in a furnace; and his voice as the sound of many waters. And he had in his right hand seven stars; and out of his mouth went a sharp two-edged sword; and his countenance was as the sun shineth in his strength. And when I saw him, I fell at his feet as dead. And he laid his right hand upon me, saying unto me, 'Fear not; I am the first and the last: I am he that liveth and was dead; and behold, I am alive forevermore, and have the keys of hell and of death." (Revelations 1:12-18) That's about as accurate a description as you're going to get of the Inner Master.

It is also stated in the Bible, "Greater is he that is in you than he that is in the world." (I John 4:4) The part of you that is spiritual is greater by far than anything of the physical world. You can take any avatar or saint or Godform as manifest in the physical world, and the part in you which is Spirit is greater than that. Jesus said, "For I say unto you, Among those that are born of women there is not a greater prophet than John the Baptist: but he that is least in the kingdom of God is greater than he." (Luke 7:28) The inner part of your consciousness is valuable beyond all measure in this world. It will transcend verbal recognition, emotional qualification, and mental imagery.

The Soul, the inner form, is so magnificent that you intuitively know its majesty even if you don't know it consciously. I sometimes think the intuitive knowledge of the Soul is part of the reason we resist and resent anyone having authority over us at any time, whether it's our parents, teachers, spouses, or employers. That part which is the Soul and the magnificence of Spirit will not be controlled or put down.

If you have a young child who resists your authority as a parent and you cannot teach the child in the discipline of this level and this life, you'll lose the child. It is your responsibility as a parent to teach your children to walk in the path of Spirit, Light and love. You must work to teach your children what they will need to know in this life. Teach them also of their Soul and Spirit, but do not allow them to default on their responsibilities to this level.

In a similar way, you must also hold yourself to the discipline of this life. Because your Soul is magnificent, you cannot assume you can run all over your fellow human beings. Remember that the inner quality of the Soul is equally beautiful in every man and woman on this planet. So you must move with loving respect through your life. Treat *everyone* with love. Be considerate and kind to all. Do you know that when you put a beggar and a millionaire side by side in Soul consciousness, you cannot tell the difference? Both are equally magnificent. A genius and one we would call mentally retarded are equal in Spirit. There is no difference. Don't put yourself up at the expense of anyone else. Recognize the oneness in Spirit.

That which is Spirit is cohesive and binds all things together in loving. Through each individual Soul, God has extended himself forward through spiritual form in organizational effort and given himself the chance to experience and express himself. It's quite obvious that some of your most dynamic experiences take place inside of you in terms of wishful thinking, fantasizing, planning, or visualizing. Therefore, the physical world often doesn't measure up to the expectation level you have built inside yourself. It seldom will measure up because inside you is the creative power of Spirit.

You are a god in your creativity, and in Spirit you have access to spiritual power. You do not necessarily have access to that spiritual power here on this level. If you can keep the two levels separated very distinctly and understand the different values of the spiritual levels and the laws governing them, you can start leading a very enchanted life. You may still turn your ankle or get a headache or have to pay car payments. Those conditions go with this level and seem to apply universally and equally. The mightiest, most powerful and wealthiest of kings or moguls are not exempt from illness or disturbance. They may think they're exempt from poverty, but they often become slaves to their wealth as they have to work harder and harder to support more and more. The man who lives in moderation, being neither wealthy nor poor, often has the greatest freedom.

Sometimes you may look at someone who appears to have their life all together and become envious, if you do not look deeper than the outer appearance. But if you could read the anguish of their secret heart, you might be filled with compassion. And you can look at people who are physically disabled and feel so sorry for them, but God may have compensated them by giving them the most joyful heart and an outlook on life filled with hope and confidence. These things really do tend to equal out as you are able to look through all the levels of Spirit. And if you cannot see all the levels, then exercise the charity and love within your heart and give nothing but love to those you meet, however their outer form appears to you in that moment.

The quality of the Soul is different than the quality of the Inner Master. They are not the same, except perhaps in the macro consciousness where there is no separation and no thing is different from another. In expression, however, the Soul is an individualized spark of the God form, and the Inner Master is an extension of the greater Master form we call the Traveler or the Christ within. God's agent has manifested itself in a very special form and has run an extension through all levels of creation and maintained it through nurturing care and loving concern. It is like an iron rod giving strength and a focus around which you can gather your energy. The Inner Master is, in essence, a rod of power. It is indeed an all-knowing, all-encompassing, and totally loving force field that knows the intimacy of your beingness. In its wisdom, it realizes the functional reality of the Soul's experience, gained as you dabble consciously in this world. The Inner Master stands back, much like a benign father, as you make your mistakes, learn your lessons, destroy, create and progress through the world.

The Inner Master is present in everyone in greater or lesser form. In those who are following a spiritual path and are consciously seeking to attune themselves to Spirit's inner guidance, the Inner Master takes on a more solid form. People who are not following a spiritual path consciously may not experience the form except as a vague ideal of conscience or sense of right and wrong. To the students and initiates of the Mystical Traveler, the Inner Master may look like the physical form of John-Roger, or it may appear in other forms as described earlier. It could also be perceived in terms of color rays and energy fields. To people who are following Hari Krishna, it may appear as the form of a man playing a flute, perhaps shaded in the color blue. The Inner Master can appear in the form of Jesus Christ if that is your attunement, or as another Master you follow as a focus in your life.

The Inner Master forms an identity level within you as something that is cognitively real. It is not a hallucination, but something you can communicate with, ask questions, and ask for guidance. It is something you can love and adore. You can also ignore it, yell at it, or criticize it, and it will continue to love you because it knows the ultimate with which you're dealing and keeps the ultimate present with you whether you're expressing and experiencing the macro or the micro consciousness. The Inner Master makes sure that you never really lose track of the vision.

Sometimes you may purposefully and responsibly turn from the Spirit and enter into a time of darkness. You may do that willfully, as a process of "doing it your way," often because you don't like anyone telling you what to do. That action can't be faulted because there is learning and growth that comes with all experience. If you don't want to do it the way suggested to you, you have a right to do it your way. If you don't know what your way is and you're just reacting against authority, it might be called stupid. And there are positive lessons in the experience of stupidity, too. In the whole field of play here, ultimately it is just God playing, and God plays all the roles.

As I work with my students from the inner level, the changes, growth and expansion of consciousness appear very natural (or perhaps supernaturally natural) as they evolve gradually from within. At some point, the student looks at everything that has shifted inside of him and says, "Of course, this is natural. I have come into sync with the way it is, not the way I thought it was or the way my parents and schoolteachers told me it would be, but the way it is." And every time you bring yourself into harmony with what is, every time reality appears and you work within its framework, you find a profound sense of freedom and a sense of your Self because you have moved past the considerations and conditions of the lower levels of consciousness and expressed from the higher levels of Spirit and Soul. The master form inside is the genius who makes harmony appear like magic. It is the Alpha and the Omega. It is behind the miracles and the phenomena. It is the formless which assumes form according to your despair or your joy.

A man who is my initiate came to me and said, "J-R, I really have made a mess of my life. I'm really in a terrible situation. I've fallen off my spiritual path and really made things very difficult for myself." I asked him, "What is it you want of me?" He said, "I guess I want assurance that everything is going to be all right." I said, "But it's not." He said, "Okay. I guess I'll have to handle it, but how bad will it get?" I said, "How bad can you imagine it will be?" He said, "Oh, God, I can think of a lot of terrible things." I said, "Like what?" He said, "Like maybe I'll go to jail for twenty years." "No," I said, "the law doesn't give that type of sentence for what you've done." He said, "It doesn't? What's the punishment?" I said, "Maybe eighteen months to five years. And if they take good behavior into consideration, you might spend less time in jail. It doesn't make a lot of sense for you to be browbeating yourself, chewing your guts into fiddle strings, kicking yourself all over the place, and gnashing your teeth when you don't know what's going to happen. Why don't you just wait and find out? What you're putting yourself through won't be counted as part of your time. The judge doesn't care if you make your life miserable before, during, or after the hearing. All he cares about are the facts, which have already taken place, so there's nothing you can do to change that. Relax, love yourself and do the best you can in the mess you've gotten yourself into. It's not going to help you to be upset, nervous, scared, panicky or anything else."

Then the fellow said, "What I really want to know is if you'll be with me spiritually while I'm going through all this?" I said, "Haven't I always been with you? What makes you think I'm not going to be with you now?" He said, "There was a time when I didn't feel you with me inwardly very much. We didn't communicate much." I asked, "Was that when you were healthy, wealthy, happy, and everything was going your way?" He said, "Yes." I said, "What did you need me for then? Everything was going so great I didn't have to bother my head with you. Everything was fine. What about when you were in trouble that other time in your life?" He said, "You were there all the time. I'd wake up and feel you with me. I'd go to sleep knowing you were there. If you hadn't been close then, I wouldn't have made it through." I said, "Yes, you would have, because all we did was strengthen the determination in you to learn and lift higher. Now you have another lesson to learn. Do more spiritual exercises. Chant your tone more. Build up all the Light units you can.

Strengthen your awareness of the rod of power present inside of you."

Use every opportunity to make your contact stronger with the Inner Master. A lot of my friends have found over the years in the course of casual conversation with me that I know what they do in their spare time and what they're talking about when they're talking behind everyone's back. Sometimes I'll mention things in passing so they will know their secrets are not so secret and need not be hidden. There is nothing you can do that has not already been done. The thing you've done which you think is so terrible that you must hide it from the world is not unique or special to you. The Inner Master knows those innermost secrets and loves you totally. Those things are the "tiddlywinks" of these lower levels. They mean nothing in Spirit.

The Inner Master is cognitively aware of and working with you all the time. Your particular experience is brought to you purposefully to strengthen you for the next experience. If you do not build strength as a progression, you will come up against a situation which requires more strength than you have, and you'll fail. Thus, what sometimes appears to be adversity can be a positive growth experience.

The Inner Master is absolutely patient, much more so than the outer form of the Traveler may be. The Traveler in outer form works with thousands of students in the very specific agreement of initiation and with millions upon millions in a more general sense. The part of the Traveler which lives with you as your Inner Master works just with you, so of course there is infinite patience there for you. That's one reason you will sometimes experience a difference between the Inner Master and the outer form of the Traveler. The outer form of the Traveler does not have less love for you, but may have less time to spend physically with you.

A long time ago when I was in India, I visited one of the swamis who had quite a following. The few people I was with had a private audience with him, and as we were leaving, he walked out with us. His followers who were outside started calling to him, asking for his attention. He stopped for one who called him, then another, another, and another. I thought, "I wonder how spiritually evolved he really is? He seems to 'jump' every time he's called. That's no way to live a life. No wonder he seems a little frazzled." I wondered if he were trying to be all things to all people in the physical level. If he were, that would be an absurd point of view. No one can do that. It was interesting that most of those who got private audiences with him thought he was magnificent. Those who didn't, didn't think he was quite so hot. And those who were sitting in the back and couldn't see him too well thought less of him. And those who fancied themselves great spiritual leaders and had sent ahead for appointments, but weren't granted time to see him, called him a fraud. And it was exactly the same person who was being perceived in all these different ways.

You must follow your own inner direction in life. If other people do not understand, their disturbance is not yours to handle. It's theirs. If you are living a life of honesty and integrity, taking care of yourself and others, not hurting yourself or anyone else, you are free to express yourself in the integrity of what you perceive as right for you. You don't have to answer to anyone else. You _do_ have to answer to the spiritual form inside of yourself, and that's easy if you are following the spiritual guidance from within.

The Inner Master speaks to you of the oneness of Spirit and the goodness of all God's creation. When you are in attunement with your guidance, you will express lovingly. You will seek to bring balance and harmony to all people and situations and lift everyone around you.

Many years ago when I was in high school, I was at the local soda fountain one evening and a fellow from my high school was there with his girl. She was really wonderful. I know because I was watching them, thinking, "What a lucky guy. Look who he's with." He was a senior, and I was only a sophomore, so I was watching him to see how he made his moves. They were having ice cream sundaes, and she said to him, "I'd like more syrup on my sundae." He said, "Sure," and turned to the waitress and said, "Could we have more syrup on her sundae?" The waitress said, "No, you've got enough!" And he said, "Could we have some more syrup? I'll be happy to pay for it." She said, "I don't care if you're going to pay for it or not; she's got enough." I wondered how he would handle that. He just turned to his girl and said, "She says you have enough." The girl said, "She's right. I've had enough." And they got up and walked out.

The waitress was also a student at our high school. So the next day I went up to her and said, "What caused you to act like that? Why wouldn't you give them more syrup?" She said, "She goes to another school, and she's dating a boy from our school." I said, "The boy you've got a crush on." She said, "That's beside the point." I said, "I think that's precisely the point. You thought life should be one way and it didn't match up. So you're going to make everyone around you pay for your illusion."

I happened to talk to the son of the man who owned the fountain a few days later and told him about the incident. His father fired the girl because after he had spoken to her, it was obvious she could not give up the negative personal point of view for the greater Spirit within. It is not a balanced action when you deny the Spirit in another human being and refuse to behave with normal consideration and concern. When you set yourself up as the supreme authority for the way life is supposed to be, you set yourself up for a fall because you deny the presence of Spirit.

I worked in hospitals for a time, and I've seen the same type of thing take place when a patient asks for something and a nurse refuses just because it doesn't happen to fit her idea of what she would like to be doing at the moment. Once I heard a patient ask for a glass of water and the nurse said, "No." I looked on the patient's chart and there was nothing written there about "no water," so I asked the doctor. He said it was fine for the patient to have water. I told him about the nurse refusing the water, and he said, "Some nurses won't do anything they don't want to do." I asked, "Then why are they nurses?" He just looked at me; there was no answer to that kind of question.

If someone asks something of you and it's not

going to hurt anyone, remember *you* are also in the other person. You can respond to the "you" in them that needs assistance. Treat people with kindness. It may be returned to you when you need it most. Never, never pass up an opportunity to assist your spiritual family, which is all mankind. When you can be of service to someone, you are—honest to God—taking care of God's business as God to God, and nothing is a greater manifestation of Spirit. You are truly blessed when you can assist another human being. You do not become less when you give to another. You gain more than you ever thought possible.

There is a guide inside you, a great counselor, a guiding Light. God is present working in you as you, pulling your consciousness away from its polarization towards the world and back into awareness of Spirit. As you move into Spirit, you're going to find there is no separation and nobody is doing it for you; it's only the "smart" part of *you* doing what the "dumb" part is too unaware to know about. You don't have to thank me or anyone else for your spiritual growth and progression, because it's only me working with me and you working with you...or more accurately, it's *us* working with *us* in the oneness of the Spirit.

One of my staff members received a letter from a relative and felt the need to respond, but he was having trouble getting his letter to say what he truly wanted it to say. He brought it to me and asked me if I would help him answer it. He showed me what he had done. He had about a page, with a lot scribbled out. I said, "I'll help you." In just a few minutes I helped him set out the main points he wanted to cover. He had his emotions so out in front of him that he couldn't get through them to the clear mental thoughts that were behind them. I didn't have the emotions running, so it was easier for me. I talked with him and explained how I read the letter from his relative as a stranger would read it, so the emotions in the letter didn't affect me or cloud the issues for me. I certainly recognized the emotions were there, but I didn't react to them. I explained to him how to read the letter point by point and then address his response to each point. And I explained to him how to keep the love present for the person who had written the letter. So his letter back to the person responded to theirs and was also permeated with spiritual love which said, in essence, "It's okay for you to express to me whatever you need to. I'll receive it in love and return only love to you."

This young man did something smart. He copied his letter down in a special notebook and said, "If I ever have to write another letter like this, I'll have reference points." That's very smart. As you find special keys that assist you, write them down in a spiritual journal or notebook. Do everything you can to assist yourself. Other people can be reference points for you, too. When you find yourself getting out of balance inside, talk with someone who can be a reference point for you and help you to come back into balance. It might be a friend, a family member, a minister, or your doctor. Take advantage of those people in your life who can assist you. There is nothing wrong with asking for help. Certainly we have all been in situations where we needed help; it's very human, and it's very nice to reach out and let someone who loves you be of service to you.

When you come into a loving and balanced place

inside yourself, it is easy to be in direct communion with the Inner Master. Through that connection, you can move into the heart of God. As you commune with the form of the Inner Master, he listens and communicates with you through intuition, inner knowing, and sometimes in words mocked up as a thought process. Be careful, however, not to deceive yourself by telling yourself what you *want* to hear and passing it off as guidance from the Inner Master. You must learn to discern the mental chatter of your mind, your wishful thinking, and your obsessive thought forms from the Inner Master's guidance. One way to check inner direction is to compare it to the outer teachings of the Traveler. The outer teachings and the inner guidance will never conflict.

The Traveler teaches three important concepts. First, use everything to your advantage. Second, take care of yourself so you can help take care of others. Third, don't hurt yourself and don't hurt others. If your inner guidance tells you to do anything that conflicts with those teachings, you are giving credence to an illusion. Study the teachings of the Traveler. Get yourself well-grounded in them. Discipline your mind so that you know the material. If you have read, studied, attended seminars and paid attention, it will be very hard for you to deceive yourself on the inner levels. And when in doubt, check it out. If you hear inner guidance that doesn't sound right to you, don't be a fool and follow it. Stop. Check it out. Find a book or tape that addresses that issue, call several people whose discernment you trust and ask them, or write directly to my office and check it out.

When you do establish contact with the Inner

Master, you are communicating so directly with Spirit that the guidance often bypasses any type of mental process. Sometimes you don't even have to ask Spirit for anything. It answers your unspoken prayer instantly. All you have to do is think something and Spirit's response comes rushing in like a wild hurricane. You say, "My God, everything is breaking loose around me. My life is opening up. All the things that I could ever dream of are happening. It's wonderful!" Yes, it is. That's the Inner Master, the Traveler, saying to you, "We're here, we're present, what can we do for you?" Be smart and ask for love to fill your life and to know the presence of God. Those are the only things that have value. Jesus said, "But seek ye first the Kingdom of God and his righteousness; and all these things shall be added unto you." (Matthew 6:33) Of course, when you discover the Kingdom of God, there is nothing on earth that can compare. What once looked very attractive isn't so tempting. When you awaken to the Inner Master and to the God of your heart, you can walk through this life and live on the earth, but you are no longer *of* the earth. You recognize its temporal nature. You move through it with detachment, looking always to Spirit for sustenance.

Where do you seek the Kingdom of God? Within yourself. Your direction, your guidance, and your fulfillment all are within you. Remember the words of John who said, "Greater is he that is in you than he that is in the world." (I John 4:4)

About the Author

Since 1963, John-Roger has traveled all over the world, lecturing, teaching, and assisting people who want to create a life of greater health, happiness, peace, and prosperity and a greater awakening to the Spirit within. His humor and practical wisdom have benefited thousands and lightened many a heart.

In the course of this work, he has given over 5,000 seminars, many of which are televised nationally on "That Which Is." He has also written more than 35 books, including co-authoring two *New York Times* best-sellers.

The common thread throughout John-Roger's work is loving, opening to the highest good of all, and the awareness that God is abundantly present and available.

If you've enjoyed this book, you may want to explore and delve more deeply into what John-Roger has shared about this subject and other related topics. See the bibliography for a selection of study materials. For an even wider selection of study materials and more information on John-Roger's teachings through MSIA, please contact us at:

MSIA®
P.O. Box 513935
Los Angeles, CA 90051-1935
(213) 737-4055
soul@msia.org
http://www.msia.org